THE KITCHEN LIBRARY

CHINESE COOKING

THE KITCHEN LIBRARY
CHINESE COOKING

Caroline Ellwood

HAMLYN

CONTENTS

This edition published in 1990 by
The Hamlyn Publishing Group Limited,
a division of the Octopus Publishing Group,
Michelin House, 81 Fulham Road,
London SW3 6RB

© Cathay Books 1982

ISBN 0 600 56931 4

Produced by Mandarin Offset
Printed and Bound in Hong Kong

NOTES

Standard spoon measurements are
used in all recipes
1 tablespoon = one 15 ml spoon
1 teaspoon = one 5 ml spoon.
All spoon measures are level.

Use freshly ground black pepper
where pepper is specified.

Ovens should be preheated to the
specified temperature.

For all recipes, quantities are given in
both metric and imperial measures.
Follow either set but not a mixture of
both, because they are not
interchangeable

Ingredients and garnishes marked
with an asterisk are explained on
pages 8-10.

INTRODUCTION

When planning a Chinese meal, the secret of success lies in choosing dishes that complement each other, yet provide contrast in texture, flavour and colour. Selecting dishes prepared by the different cooking methods is also important for variety.

Party meals are elaborate in China, consisting of numerous courses. They include hors d'oeuvres of various meats, seafoods and marinated vegetables; quick-fried foods and soup. These all precede the special main dish, which might be Peking duck or Red-cooked lamb, served with accompaniments and rice.

A good Chinese family meal also provides a wide variety of dishes but all the dishes are placed on the table together. The meal usually consists of a main dish, one or two quick-fried recipes, and steamed – rather than fried – rice.

Our meals, of course, are more simple affairs but the same basic rules should apply, even on a small scale. When planning a meal just for two, include one main dish, one vegetable dish, a soup and a rice dish. When cooking for more people increase the number and variety of dishes, as described above, rather than the quantity of each dish. The more variety – the more successful the meal!

REGIONAL COOKING

There are four principal schools of Chinese cuisine: Cantonese (Kwangtung province), Huaiyang, Szechuan and Peking. Each region has its own specialities which depend on the climate and availability of local produce.

Cantonese cooking is influenced by the availability of locally caught fish, and seafood specialities are numerous. Stuffed vegetables are popular, often using shellfish for the filling. It is also from Canton that the delicious crispy pork recipes originate.

Huaiyang, with its centre at Yangchow, provides many of the steamed dishes, including savoury dumplings. The subtle-flavoured noodle recipes come from the banks of the Yangtze river delta in this area. Also in eastern China is Nanking, known for its duck dishes, and Shanghai – the trading centre – which has its own sophisticated cuisine.

In contrast, food from the Szechuan area is richly flavoured and piquant. Characteristic Szechuan dishes tend to be hot and peppery, mainly due to the use of chilli peppers, hot pepper oil and Szechuan peppercorns.

The Peking cuisine is the most varied of all. Over the centuries chefs from the different regions of China have brought their own specialities to the capital city making it the culinary centre. At the same time, Peking has its own cuisine; it is from here that the famous Peking Duck and Mongolian Hot Pot originate. The northern province of Honan on the Hwang Ho (Yellow River) is famous for its sweet-sour dishes.

PREPARING INGREDIENTS

In Chinese cooking the emphasis is on the preparation of food rather than cooking. This is the time-consuming part of the recipe – the actual cooking time is very short. Great care should be taken when cutting to ensure that all ingredients are a similar size and will therefore cook evenly.

Meat should be cut across the grain to help tenderise it. Normally, it is either sliced or shredded. Vegetables may be sliced straight or diagonally, shredded or diced.

To slice a vegetable diagonally, hold the knive or cleaver at a 45° angle to the vegetable, with the blade pointing away from you. To shred a vegetable, cut into diagonal slices, then into thin strips. To dice, simply cut the food into 1 cm (½ inch) cubes. Always prepare each ingredient and put on one side before starting to cook.

COOKING METHODS AND EQUIPMENT

Frying, steaming and braising are the common methods.
Stir-frying This is the most common Chinese cooking

method. As the name implies, it is a technique of frying foods over a high heat, stirring constantly.

A small amount of oil is used and the food is stirred vigorously and constantly throughout cooking, which only takes a few minutes. This method ensures that the food is sealed and cooked quickly to hold in the flavour. A wok, with its round base and sloping sides, is perfect for stir-frying. If a wok is unavailable, use a deep frying pan instead.

Deep-frying A wok or deep-fryer can be used for this method. The food is normally dipped into a batter of some sort before frying in hot oil. It is advisable to use a fat thermometer to check the temperature of the oil.

Steaming Chinese steamers are made from bamboo in varying sizes to fit inside a wok or over a saucepan. They have a bamboo lid and are designed so that steam passes through the tiny holes in the bamboo to cook the food.

The food is arranged on an ovenproof plate, which is then placed on the perforated base of the steamer.

It is possible to use a metal steamer on top of a saucepan for smaller items, but bamboo steamers are readily available at reasonable cost and are worth buying.

Red braising This is a unique Chinese style of cooking. The food is stewed in a mixture of soy sauce, water and sugar, with flavourings of root ginger, spring onions and sherry. The food takes on a reddish colour during cooking.

SPECIALIST INGREDIENTS

The following ingredients are available from Chinese food stores, some supermarkets, delicatessens and greengrocers.

Abalone: A smooth-textured shellfish available in cans.

Bamboo Shoots: Crunchy cream-coloured shoots of the bamboo plant. Available in canned and dried form. (Dried bamboo shoots should be soaked before use.)

Bean Curd: Made from ground soya beans, curd is pressed and set into cakes, 7.5 cm (3 inches) square. Fresh bean curd should be eaten on day of purchase. Long-life bean curd, 'tofu', is available in cartons.

Bean Paste, Sweet: Thick, red soy bean paste with added sugar, sold in cans. Used as a dip and as a base for sweet sauces.

Bean Sauce, Yellow/Black: A thick sauce made from black or yellow soy beans, sold in cans.

Bean Sprouts: Tiny, crunchy shoots of mung beans. Bean sprouts are available fresh and should be eaten on day of purchase. Also sold in cans, but fresh ones are recommended.

Black Beans: Salted, fermented black beans with a strong, salty flavour. Sold in packs or by weight. Must be soaked for 5 to 10 minutes before use.

Chestnuts, Dried: Require soaking before use. Fresh chestnuts may be used instead, without soaking.

Chinese Cabbage: Also called Chinese celery cabbage, it has a slightly sweet flavour. Can be eaten raw in salads, or cooked.

Chinese Mushrooms, Dried: Need to be soaked in warm water for 15 to 20 minutes and stalks must be removed before use. Continental dried mushrooms can be used instead.

Coriander: Also called Chinese parsley, it is a distinctive flavoured herb. Parsley may be substituted, but it does not impart the same flavour.

Five Spice Powder: A mixture of five spices – anise pepper, star anise, cinnamon, cloves and fennel seeds. It is strong and pungent and should be used sparingly. Sold in ready mixed and powder form.

Ginger Root: Should be peeled before use, then crushed or shredded. For 1 piece root ginger, cut a piece roughly 2.5 cm (1 inch) square.

Hoisin Sauce: A thick, brownish-red soy-based sauce. Used as a condiment and in cooked dishes.

Hot Pepper Oil: A hot tasting oil, made from hot chillies.

Lotus Leaves: Used as a wrapping for foods to be cooked to impart flavour. Dried lotus leaves are sold in packages; soak in warm water for 20 minutes before use.

Oyster Sauce: A light sauce made from oysters and soy sauce. Used for flavouring meat and vegetables.

Peppercorns, Szechuan: Used whole or ground, in marinades and cooked dishes.

Pickled Cabbage: Usually yellow-green in colour, packed in brine in jars.

Pickled Vegetables, Szechuan: Hot and spicy in flavour, they are added to meat, fish and vegetable dishes.

Rice Stick Noodles: These are long sticks, like noodles, made from rice flour. They do not require soaking before use.

Sesame Seed Oil: A nutty-flavoured oil, generally used in small quantities at the end of cooking.

Sesame Seed Paste: Rather like peanut butter in texture and flavour.

Sesame Seeds: Tiny, flat seeds, used in both sweet and savoury recipes; often roasted.

Shrimps, Dried: These have a strong, salty flavour.

Soy Sauce: The common dark variety is used unless otherwise stated. Light soy sauce is often used as an accompaniment.

Straw Mushrooms: Small round type of mushroom. Available in cans.

Transparent Noodles: Also called cellophane noodles, these are semi-transparent. Soak in hot water for 5 minutes before use.

Water Chestnuts: Available in cans, these have a crunchy texture.

Water Chestnut Flour: Made from water chestnuts, this has a distinctive flavour.

Wonton Skins: Thin yellow dough, packed in cellophane.

Wooden Ears: Black fungi with a delicate flavour. Soak in warm water for 20 minutes before use.

GARNISHES

Garnishes are frequently used to add colour to Chinese dishes. Those described below are simple to make.

Radish Flowers: Trim each end of the radish. Using a sharp knife, make 'V' cuts around the top and remove the cut parts to expose the white of the radish.

Radish Roses: Cut small petals all around the radish; chill in iced water until the petals open.

Spring Onion Brushes: Trim the green top and remove the white part. Carefully shred the top leaving 2.5 cm (1 inch) attached at the base. Immerse in iced water until the spring onion opens out and curls.

Carrot Flowers: Trim the ends. Using a sharp knife, make 'V' cuts along the carrot. Cut across into slices.

Cucumber Fans: Cut a 7.5 cm (3 inch) piece from the rounded end of a cucumber. Cut in half lengthways. Cut each half into strips to within 1 cm (½ inch) from the end, then trim each strip, removing excess flesh, to about 3 mm (¼ inch) thickness. Carefully turn alternative strips up to the uncut end, as illustrated. Use at once.

Tomato Flowers: Thinly pare all the skin from the tomato, taking care to keep it in one piece. Tightly curl the skin into a circle as shown. Use at once.

   Turnip, carrot and apple flowers can be prepared this way.

Chilli Flowers: Cut the chilli lengthwise into quarters to within 1 cm (½ inch) from the stem end, taking care not to remove the seeds. Shred each quarter of chilli leaving the base attached. Place in iced water for about 1 hour to open.

STOCK

Stock is an essential ingredient in many Chinese recipes and its flavour is important – particularly in soups and braised dishes. Use home-made stock whenever possible for the best flavour. If you haven't time to make your own stock, canned consommé makes an excellent substitute. Stock cubes are less suitable – they tend to be too salty when used in combination with Chinese flavourings, such as soy sauce.

Chicken stock: Immerse a chicken carcass in a pan of boiling water for 2 minutes. Discard the water and return the bones to the pan. Add 2 chopped onions, 3-4 chopped carrots, 2 garlic cloves, 8 peppercorns, ½ teaspoon salt and a bouquet garni. Pour in 2 litres (3½ pints) cold water, bring slowly to the boil and skim the surface. Cover and simmer for 3½ to 4 hours. Strain through a fine sieve and allow to cool. Store, covered, in the refrigerator for up to 3 days. Remove any fat from the surface before use.

Meat stock: Prepare as above, using 1.75 kg (4 lb) beef, veal or pork bones in place of the chicken carcass.

SOUPS

Egg Flower Soup

4-5 wooden ears*
  (optional)
2 tablespoons soy
  sauce
2 teaspoons cornflour
175 g (6 oz) pork
  fillet, shredded
900 ml (1½ pints)
  stock
1 teaspoon salt
2 eggs
2 spring onions,
  chopped
1 tablespoon chopped
  coriander*

Soak the wooden ears in warm water, if using, for 10 minutes. Rinse and drain well, then chop roughly.

Blend the soy sauce and cornflour together. Add the pork and toss until evenly coated. Bring the stock to the boil, add the salt, pork and wooden ears, if using, and cook for 5 minutes.

Beat the eggs until frothy and pour into the boiling stock, stirring constantly. Remove from the heat, add the spring onions and coriander and serve immediately.

Serves 4 to 6

Soup with Beef Balls

4-5 dried Chinese
  mushrooms*
350 g (12 oz) lean
  beef, minced
1 onion, finely
  chopped
salt
1 tablespoon
  cornflour
1 small egg
900 ml (1½ pints)
  beef stock
1 bunch watercress,
  stalks removed
3 spring onions,
  finely chopped
1 tablespoon soy
  sauce

Soak the mushrooms in warm water for 15 minutes. Squeeze dry and discard the hard stalks, then slice the mushroom caps.

Mix the beef, onion, salt to taste, cornflour and egg together and shape the mixture into small balls. Drop the meat balls into iced water for 15 minutes; drain thoroughly.

Meanwhile, heat the stock in a large pan. Add the meat balls and cook for 10 minutes. Add the mushrooms, watercress, spring onions and soy sauce and cook for 2 minutes. Serve hot.

Serves 4 to 6

Hot Peppery Soup

2 cakes bean curd*
2 tablespoons oil
2 red or green
    chillies, seeded and
    chopped
125 g (4 oz) chicken
    breast, minced
1 tablespoon
    cornflour
8 crisp lettuce leaves
900 ml (1½ pints)
    chicken stock
2 tablespoons soy
    sauce
2 spring onions,
    chopped
125 g (4 oz) frozen
    peeled prawns,
    thawed
1 tablespoon cider
    vinegar
pepper

Cut each bean curd cake into 10 pieces. Heat the oil in a wok or frying pan, add the chillies and fry briskly for about 30 seconds to extract all the oil and flavour; discard the chillies. Add the bean curd to the pan and fry for 3 to 4 minutes until golden brown. Drain and set aside.

Mix the chicken and cornflour together. Tear each lettuce leaf into 3 or 4 pieces.

Heat the stock in a large pan. Add the chicken and cornflour mixture and stir until evenly mixed. Add the lettuce, soy sauce, spring onions, prawns and cider vinegar. Bring to the boil, then add pepper to taste. Cook for 2 minutes. Add the bean curd and serve hot.

Serves 4 to 6

Sweetcorn and Prawn Soup

2 teaspoons finely
    chopped root
    ginger*
1 tablespoon dry
    sherry
250 g (8 oz) frozen
    peeled prawns,
    thawed
900 ml (1½ pints)
    chicken stock
1 x 326 g (11½ oz)
    can sweetcorn
salt
50 g (2 oz) lean
    ham, diced
1 tablespoon chopped
    chives

Mix the ginger, sherry and prawns together. Bring the stock to the boil, then stir in the prawn mixture. Drain the sweetcorn and add to the pan with salt to taste. Cook for 2 minutes, stirring occasionally.

Sprinkle with the ham and chives and serve immediately.

Serves 4 to 6

Pork Spare Ribs Soup

500 g (1 lb) pork
  spare ribs
1 tablespoon oil
2 teaspoons shredded
  root ginger*
1 clove garlic, sliced
2 spring onions,
  chopped
900 ml (1½ pints)
  beef stock
1 teaspoon salt
2 tomatoes, diced
250 g (8 oz) bean
  sprouts*

Cut the spare ribs into 2.5 cm
(1 inch) pieces.

Heat the oil in a pan, add the spare
ribs and fry for 5 minutes until
golden brown. Add the ginger, garlic
and spring onions and cook for
2 minutes. Add the stock and bring
to the boil. Cover and simmer for
1 hour or until the meat is tender.

Add the remaining ingredients and
cook for 1 minute. Serve hot.
Serves 4 to 6

15

Hot and Sour Soup

4 dried Chinese
  mushrooms*
2 celery sticks
900 ml (1½ pints)
  stock
175 g (6 oz)
  shrimps, fresh or
  frozen and thawed
50 g (2 oz)
  Szechuan pickled
  vegetables*, sliced
50 g (2 oz) canned
  bamboo shoots*,
  drained and
  shredded
½ cucumber
2 tablespoons sherry
2 tablespoons soy
  sauce
1 tablespoon red
  wine vinegar
25 g (1 oz) ham,
  diced
1 spring onion,
  chopped

Soak the mushrooms in warm water for 15 minutes. Squeeze dry, discard the hard stalks, then slice the mushroom caps. Slice the celery sticks diagonally.

Bring the stock to the boil, add the shrimps, pickled vegetables, bamboo shoots, mushrooms and celery and simmer for 5 minutes.

Cut the cucumber into 5 cm (2 inch) matchstick lengths. Add to the pan with the sherry, soy sauce, vinegar and ham and cook for 1 minute. Sprinkle with the spring onion and serve immediately.

Serves 4 to 6

Clam and Abalone Soup with Chinese Mushrooms

8-10 dried Chinese
   mushrooms*
1.2 litres (2 pints)
   stock
50 g (2 oz)
   abalone*, thinly
   sliced
125 g (4 oz) chicken
   breast, thinly
   sliced
1 piece root ginger*,
   diced
1-2 tablespoons dry
   sherry
1 tablespoon soy
   sauce
1 x 227 g (8 oz) can
   clams, drained
chopped spring onion
   to garnish

Soak the mushrooms in warm water for 15 minutes. Squeeze dry and discard the hard stalks, then cut the mushroom caps into quarters.

Bring the stock to the boil and add the abalone, chicken and ginger. Simmer for 2 minutes, add the remaining ingredients and cook for 2 minutes.

Sprinkle with the spring onion and serve immediately.

Serves 4 to 6

Shredded Pork and Noodles in Soup

3-4 dried Chinese
   mushrooms*
   (optional)
250 g (8 oz) lean
   pork, shredded
1 tablespoon soy
   sauce
1 tablespoon dry
   sherry
350 g (12 oz) egg
   noodles
900 ml (1 ½ pints)
   stock
4 spring onions,
   chopped
125 g (4 oz) canned
   bamboo shoots*,
   drained and
   shredded
few Chinese cabbage
   leaves*, shredded

Soak the mushrooms in warm water for 15 minutes, if using. Squeeze dry, discard the hard stalks, then slice the mushroom caps.

Put the pork in a bowl, add the soy sauce and sherry and leave to marinate for 10 to 15 minutes.

Cook the noodles in boiling salted water for about 5 minutes, or until cooked; drain.

Bring the stock to the boil, add the mushrooms, if using, pork, marinade, spring onions and bamboo shoots. Simmer for 2 to 3 minutes, then add the noodles and cabbage. Cook for 2 minutes. Serve hot.
Serves 4 to 6

Velvet Chicken and Mushroom Soup

175 g (6 oz) chicken
   breast
1 egg white
2 teaspoons cornflour
900 ml (1 ½ pints)
   chicken stock
50 g (2 oz) button
   mushrooms, sliced
75 g (3 oz) canned
   bamboo shoots*,
   drained and
   shredded
1 teaspoon finely
   chopped root
   ginger*
2 spring onions,
   chopped
½ teaspoon salt
1 tablespoon soy sauce

Cut the chicken into matchstick pieces. Put the egg white and cornflour in a bowl and mix well. Add the chicken and toss until evenly coated.

Bring the stock to the boil, add the chicken and remaining ingredients and simmer for 3 minutes. Serve hot.
Serves 4 to 6

Pure Vegetable Soup

4 dried Chinese
   mushrooms*
25 g (1 oz)
   transparent
   noodles*
½ bunch watercress
900 ml (1½ pints)
   stock
2 courgettes, diced
1 small turnip, diced
50 g (2 oz) spinach,
   chopped
2 carrots, diced
1 teaspoon salt
1 tablespoon soy
   sauce
2 spring onions,
   chopped

Soak the mushrooms in warm water for 15 minutes. Squeeze dry and discard the hard stalks, then slice the mushroom caps.

Soak the noodles in hot water for 10 minutes; drain. Remove the stalks from the watercress and divide the leaves.

Bring the stock to the boil. Add the courgettes, turnip, watercress, spinach and carrots. Simmer for 20 minutes.

Add the remaining ingredients and cook for 5 minutes. Serve hot.
Serves 4 to 6

FISH & SHELLFISH

Deep-Fried Scallops

12 scallops, fresh or
  frozen and thawed
1/2 teaspoon very
  finely chopped root
  ginger*
2 spring onions,
  finely chopped
3 tablespoons
  self-raising flour
pinch of salt
2 teaspoons dry
  sherry
1 egg, beaten
oil for deep-frying
TO GARNISH:
tomato flower*
coriander leaves*

Cut the scallops in half. Parcook fresh ones in boiling water for 1 minute; drain thoroughly. Mix the scallops with the ginger and spring onions.

Put the flour and salt in a bowl, add the sherry and egg and beat to a smooth batter. Fold in the scallops and toss until evenly coated.

Heat the oil in a wok or deep-fryer to 160°C (325°F) and deep-fry the scallops for 2 to 3 minutes until golden brown. Drain on kitchen paper.

Arrange on a warmed serving dish and garnish with a tomato flower and coriander leaves. Serve immediately.

Serves 4

Quick-Fried Prawns

125 g (4 oz) fresh
  asparagus, cut into
  2.5 cm (1 inch)
  pieces (optional)
4 tablespoons dry
  sherry
1 egg white
pinch of salt
500 g (1 lb) peeled
  prawns, fresh or
  frozen and thawed
1 tablespoon oil
1 teaspoon finely
  chopped root
  ginger*
2 spring onions,
  chopped

Cook the asparagus in boiling salted water for 5 minutes, if using; drain thoroughly.

Mix 2 tablespoons of the sherry with the egg white and salt. Add the prawns and toss until evenly coated; drain.

Heat the oil in a wok or frying pan, add the ginger and half of the spring onions and fry for 2 minutes. Add the prawns and cook for 5 minutes, or until they become pink. Add the asparagus, if using, and remaining sherry and cook for 1 minute.

Transfer to a warmed serving dish and sprinkle with the remaining spring onion. Serve immediately.
Serves 4 to 6

Quick-Fried Squid with Crab and Tomato Sauce

500 g (1 lb) cleaned
   squid, fresh or
   frozen and thawed
1 tablespoon oil
2 pieces root ginger*,
   finely chopped
3 spring onions,
   finely chopped
1 x 177 g (6 oz) can
   crabmeat
1 x 65 g (2¼ oz)
   can tomato purée
1 teaspoon sugar
1 tablespoon light
   soy sauce*
4 tablespoons chicken
   stock
1 tablespoon dry
   sherry
2 teaspoons cornflour
chopped spring onion
   to garnish

Cut the squid into 2.5 cm (1 inch) pieces.

Heat the oil in a wok or deep frying pan, add the ginger and spring onions and stir-fry for 1 minute. Add the squid and cook for 2 minutes. Add the remaining ingredients, except the cornflour, and mix well. Cook for 2 minutes, stirring.

Blend the cornflour to a smooth paste with 1 tablespoon water. Stir into the pan and cook, stirring, until thickened.

Spoon into a warmed serving dish, garnish with spring onion and serve immediately.

Serves 4 to 6

Steamed Sweet and Sour Fish

1 large whole plaice,
   cleaned
salt
2 pieces root ginger*,
   shredded
3 spring onions,
   sliced
SAUCE:
150 ml (¼ pint) fish
   or chicken stock
1 tablespoon soy
   sauce
1 tablespoon sugar
1 tablespoon wine
   vinegar
1 tablespoon dry
   sherry
1 tablespoon tomato
   purée
1 teaspoon chilli
   sauce
pinch of salt
1 tablespoon
   cornflour
TO GARNISH:
coriander leaves*
tomato flowers*

Score the fish by making 3 diagonal cuts on each side. Rub the fish with salt and sprinkle with the ginger and spring onions. Put on an ovenproof plate and place in a steamer. Steam for 12 to 15 minutes until tender.

Meanwhile, make the sauce. Mix all the ingredients, except the cornflour, together in a small saucepan, bring to the boil and cook for 1 minute. Blend the cornflour with 2 tablespoons water and stir into the sauce. Cook, stirring, until thickened.

Carefully lift the plaice onto a warmed serving dish. Spoon over the sauce and serve hot, garnished with coriander and tomato flowers.

Serves 4

NOTE: Fresh or frozen plaice can be used.

Braised Fish with Black Bean Sauce

3 tablespoons black
  beans*
2 tablespoons oil
2 spring onions,
  chopped
1 piece root ginger*,
  finely chopped
1 small red pepper,
  cored, seeded and
  diced
2 celery sticks,
  chopped
2 tablespoons soy
  sauce
2 tablespoons dry
  sherry
4 cod or haddock
  cutlets, each
  weighing 150 g
  (5 oz)
shredded spring onion
  to garnish

Soak the black beans in warm water for 10 minutes; drain.

Heat the oil in a wok or deep frying pan, add the spring onions, ginger, red pepper and celery and stir-fry for 1 minute. Stir in the soy sauce and sherry. Place the fish on top of the vegetables and simmer for 5 to 10 minutes until almost tender, depending on the thickness of the fish. Spoon over the black beans and cook for 2 minutes.

Arrange the fish on a warmed serving dish and spoon the sauce over. Serve hot, garnished with spring onion.
Serves 4

Eggs Fu-Yung

3 dried Chinese
  mushrooms*
2 tablespoons oil
3 spring onions
1 piece root ginger*
1 clove garlic, crushed
25 g (1 oz) canned
  bamboo shoots*,
  drained and diced
6 canned water
  chestnuts, drained
  and chopped*
  (optional)
25 g (1 oz) frozen
  peeled prawns,
  thawed
1 x 177 g (6 oz) can
  crabmeat, drained
1 tablespoon dry
  sherry
salt
6 eggs, beaten
TO GARNISH:
radish flower*
cucumber twist

Soak the dried mushrooms in warm
water for 15 minutes. Squeeze dry
and discard the hard stalks, then
chop the mushroom caps. Chop the
spring onions and ginger finely.

Heat the oil in a wok or deep
frying pan, add the spring onions,
ginger and garlic and stir-fry for
1 minute. Add the mushrooms,
bamboo shoots and water chestnuts,
if using, and cook for 30 seconds.

Stir in the prawns, crabmeat and
sherry and season liberally with salt.
Lower the heat and pour in the
beaten eggs. Scramble until the
mixture is just set.

Pile onto a warmed serving dish
and serve immediately, garnished
with the radish flower and cucumber
twist.

Serves 4 to 6

Trout with Salted Cabbage

2 tablespoons oil
1 onion, chopped
2 pieces root ginger*,
    finely shredded
4 trout, cleaned
150 ml (¼ pint)
    chicken stock
25 g (1 oz) pickled
    cabbage*, chopped
25 g (1 oz) canned
    bamboo shoots*,
    drained and sliced
1 tablespoon soy
    sauce
2 teaspoons dry
    sherry
TO GARNISH:
lemon twists
coriander leaves*

Heat the oil in a wok or deep frying pan, add the onion and ginger and cook for 1 minute. Add the trout and fry for 1 minute on each side, until browned.

Stir in the stock, then add the cabbage, bamboo shoots, soy sauce and sherry. Cook for 10 minutes, basting the fish occasionally.

Transfer to a warmed serving dish and garnish with lemon twists and coriander. Serve immediately.
Serves 4

Five-Willows Fish

1 small cucumber
2 carrots
1 piece root ginger*,
    sliced
3 spring onions,
    chopped
2 cloves garlic,
    1 crushed and
    1 sliced
120 ml (4 fl oz)
    vinegar
1 grey mullet, carp
    or bass, cleaned
4 tablespoons oil
1 tablespoon hoisin
    sauce*
2 tablespoons sugar
1 tablespoon sesame
    seed oil*
TO GARNISH:
cucumber fan*
carrot flower*

Cut the cucumber in half lengthways and discard the soft centre. Slice the cucumber flesh and carrots into 5 cm (2 inch) long matchstick pieces.

Put the cucumber, carrots, ginger, spring onions, crushed garlic and vinegar in a bowl and mix well. Leave to marinate for 30 minutes.

Score the fish by making 3 diagonal cuts on both sides. Heat the oil in a wok or deep frying pan, add the sliced garlic and fry for 1 minute. Add the fish and fry for 1 minute on each side until golden brown.

Add the vegetables and marinade, stir in the hoisin sauce and sugar and cook for 2 minutes; sprinkle with the sesame seed oil.

Transfer the fish to a warmed serving dish and spoon over the vegetables and sauce. Garnish with the cucumber fan and carrot flower and serve immediately.
Serves 4 to 6

CHICKEN & DUCK DISHES

Deep-Fried Chicken Legs

2 tablespoons sherry
2 tablespoons soy
  sauce
1 teaspoon sugar
1 piece root ginger*,
  finely chopped
2 cloves garlic, crushed
8 chicken drumsticks
50 g (2 oz) plain
  flour
1-2 eggs, beaten
oil for deep-frying
TO GARNISH:
radish flowers*
chilli flowers*
cucumber slices

Put the sherry, soy sauce, sugar, ginger and garlic in a bowl and mix well. Add the drumsticks, turn to coat and leave to marinate for 1 hour. Remove the chicken and reserve the marinade.

Put the flour in a bowl, beat in the egg, then gradually mix in the marinade, stirring well to form a smooth paste. Dip the chicken into the mixture and turn to coat evenly.

Heat the oil in a wok or deep-fryer and deep-fry the chicken legs for 12 to 15 minutes until golden brown. Drain on kitchen paper.

Serve hot, garnished with radish flowers, placed in chilli flowers, and cucumber slices.
Serves 4 to 6

Braised Chicken with Peppers and Corn

1 tablespoon oil
3 spring onions,
    chopped
2 pieces root ginger*,
    shredded
500 g (1 lb) boned
    chicken breast,
    shredded
2 tablespoons light
    soy sauce*
2 tablespoons dry
    sherry
2 green peppers,
    cored, seeded and
    sliced
1 x 425 g (15 oz)
    can baby corn or
    sweetcorn, drained

Heat the oil in a wok or frying pan, add the spring onions and ginger and fry for 1 minute. Add the chicken and brown lightly. Pour in the soy sauce and sherry and cook for a further 1 minute. Stir in the peppers and corn and stir-fry for 2 minutes.

Pile the mixture onto a warmed serving dish and serve immediately.
Serves 4 to 6

Chicken Wings with Oyster Sauce

500 g (1 lb) chicken
wings
4 spring onions,
chopped
1 piece root ginger*,
shredded
1 clove garlic, sliced
1 tablespoon soy
sauce
2 tablespoons dry
sherry
2 tablespoons oil
2 leeks, sliced
3 tablespoons oyster
sauce*
TO GARNISH:
radish flowers*
cucumber slices

Trim the tips off the chicken wings,
then cut the wings in half at the
joints.

Put the spring onions, ginger,
garlic, soy sauce and sherry in a
bowl. Add the chicken wings and
stir well to coat, then leave to
marinate for 15 minutes.

Heat the oil in a wok or deep
frying pan, add the chicken and
marinade and stir-fry for 15 minutes.
Add the leeks and oyster sauce and
cook for a further 3 to 4 minutes.

Serve immediately, garnished with
radish flowers and cucumber slices.

Serves 4 to 6

Lemon Chicken

2 tablespoons dry
  sherry
4 spring onions,
  chopped
1 piece root ginger*,
  shredded
500 g (1 lb) boned
  chicken, shredded
2 tablespoons oil
2 celery sticks, sliced
125 g (4 oz) button
  mushrooms,
  quartered
1 green pepper,
  cored, seeded and
  sliced
2 tablespoons light
  soy sauce
shredded rind of
  2 lemons
lemon slices to
  garnish

Put the sherry, spring onions and
ginger in a bowl. Add the chicken,
toss well to coat, and leave to
marinate for 15 minutes.

Heat the oil in a wok or deep
frying pan. Add the celery,
mushrooms and green pepper and
stir-fry for 1 minute. Add the
chicken and marinade and cook for
3 minutes. Stir in the soy sauce and
lemon rind and cook for a further
minute.

Pile into a warmed serving dish,
garnish with lemon slices and serve
immediately.

Serves 4 to 6

Chicken with Cashew Nuts

3 tablespoons dry
   sherry
1 egg white
1 teaspoon cornflour
2 boned chicken
   breasts, cut into
   small pieces
2 tablespoons oil
2 spring onions,
   chopped
1 green pepper,
   cored, seeded and
   diced
125 g (4 oz) canned
   bamboo shoots*,
   drained and shredded
1 tablespoon soy
   sauce
125 g (4 oz)
   unsalted cashew
   nuts

Mix 2 tablespoons of the sherry, the
egg white and cornflour together.
Add the chicken and toss well until
evenly coated.

Heat the oil in a wok or frying
pan, add the spring onions and
stir-fry for 30 seconds. Add the
chicken and cook for 3 minutes. Add
the remaining ingredients and cook
for 2 minutes.

Pile into a warmed serving dish
and serve immediately.
Serves 4

Chicken in Foil

1 tablespoon soy
   sauce
1 tablespoon dry
   sherry
1 tablespoon sesame
   seed oil*
500 g (1 lb) boned
   chicken breast, cut
   into 16 equal
   pieces
4 spring onions, each
   cut into 4 pieces
2 pieces root ginger*,
   shredded
1 celery stick,
   shredded

Mix the soy sauce, sherry and sesame
seed oil together. Add the chicken
and toss well to coat, then leave to
marinate for 15 to 20 minutes.

Cut out 16 pieces of foil large
enough to enclose the pieces of
chicken generously. Brush the foil
with oil, place a piece of chicken in
the centre and top with a piece of
spring onion, some ginger and
celery. Fold the foil over to enclose
the chicken and seal the edges well.
Place in a steamer and steam for
10 to 12 minutes.

Serve hot in the foil.
Serves 4 to 6

Chicken with Chestnuts

125 g (4 oz) dried
  chestnuts*
500 g (1 lb) boned
  chicken breast
1/2 teaspoon salt
2 tablespoons oil
2 cloves garlic, sliced
1 piece root ginger*,
  finely chopped
4 spring onions, each
  cut into 4 pieces
2 tablespoons soy
  sauce
2 tablespoons sherry
2 teaspoons sugar
1 tablespoon
  cornflour

Soak the chestnuts in warm water for 1 hour; drain. Cut the chicken into cubes and toss in the salt.

Heat the oil in a wok or frying pan, add the garlic and fry until browned. Add the ginger, spring onions and chicken and stir-fry for 1 minute. Add the chestnuts and cook for 2 minutes. Add the soy sauce, sherry and sugar.

Blend the cornflour with 2 tablespoons water. Stir into the pan and cook, stirring, for 1 minute.

Spoon into a warmed serving dish and serve immediately.

Serves 4 to 6

NOTE: Fresh cooked chestnuts may be used in place of soaked dried ones.

Diced Chicken with Chillies

2 tablespoons oil
1 clove garlic, sliced
350 g (12 oz) boned
   chicken breast,
   diced
1 red pepper, cored,
   seeded and diced
2 green chillies,
   seeded and sliced
50 g (2 oz) bean
   sprouts*
2 tablespoons soy
   sauce
2 tablespoons chilli
   sauce
coriander leaves* to
   garnish

Heat the oil in a wok or frying pan, add the garlic and fry for 1 minute. Add the chicken and stir-fry for 1 minute. Add the pepper and chillies and cook for a further minute. Stir in the bean sprouts, soy sauce and chilli sauce and cook for 2 minutes.

Turn into a warmed serving dish, garnish with coriander and serve immediately.
Serves 4

Chicken in Sesame Sauce

500 g (1 lb) boned
   chicken breast
1 tablespoon oil
125 g (4 oz)
   unsalted cashew
   nuts
75 g (3 oz) canned
   straw mushrooms*
MARINADE:
3 spring onions,
   chopped
3 tablespoons soy
   sauce
2 tablespoons each
   hot pepper oil*
   and sesame seed
   oil*
1 tablespoon sesame
   seed paste*
1 teaspoon ground
   Szechuan
   peppercorns*

Put the marinade ingredients in a
bowl. Cut the chicken into cubes,
then add to the marinade, turning to
coat thoroughly. Leave to marinate
for 30 minutes.

Meanwhile, heat the oil in a wok
or frying pan, add the cashew nuts
and fry until golden brown. Drain
on kitchen paper.

Add the chicken and marinade to
the pan and stir-fry for 2 minutes.
Drain the mushrooms, halve and add
to the pan. Cook for a further
minute. Pile the mixture onto a
warmed serving dish and sprinkle
with the nuts. Serve immediately.
Serves 4 to 6

Pleasure-Boat Duck

1 x 1.75 kg (4 lb)
  oven-ready duck
4 dried Chinese
  mushrooms*
2 tablespoons oil
4 spring onions,
  chopped
1 piece root ginger*,
  finely chopped
125 g (4 oz) lean
  pork, shredded
50 g (2 oz) broad
  beans, cooked

GLAZE:
3 tablespoons soy
  sauce
1 tablespoon dry
  sherry
1 tablespoon sesame
  seed oil*

TO GARNISH:
turnip flowers*
radishes
mint leaves

Immerse the duck in a pan of boiling water for 2 minutes, then drain well.

Soak the dried mushrooms in warm water for 15 minutes. Squeeze dry, discard the hard stalks, then slice the mushroom caps.

Heat the oil in a wok or frying pan, add the spring onions, ginger and pork and fry for 2 minutes. Add the beans and cook for a further minute. Add the mushrooms.

Leave to cool, then use to stuff the duck; sew up securely.

Mix the glaze ingredients together and brush over the duck. Place in a roasting pan and cook in a preheated hot oven, 220°C (425°F), Gas Mark 7, for 1¼ to 1½ hours, basting occasionally with the glaze.

Transfer to a warmed serving dish and garnish with turnip flowers, with radish centres, and mint leaves. Serve immediately.

Serves 4 to 6

Soy-Braised Duck

1 x 1.5-1.75 kg
  (3-4 lb)
  oven-ready duck
4 pieces root ginger*
1 large onion
1 teaspoon salt
6 tablespoons soy
  sauce
3 tablespoons malt
  vinegar
1 tablespoon oil
4 spring onions, each
  cut into 3 pieces
150 ml (¼ pint)
  chicken stock
1 x 227 g (8 oz) can
  pineapple slices,
  halved
3 tablespoons dry
  sherry
1 tablespoon
  cornflour, blended
  with 2 tablespoons
  water
TO GARNISH:
pineapple slices
shredded spring onions

Prick the skin of the duck all over.
Finely chop the ginger and onion.
Mix with the salt and rub inside the
duck. Put in a large bowl and add
the soy sauce and vinegar. Leave
for 1 hour, basting occasionally.

Transfer to a roasting pan. Cook
in a preheated hot oven, 220°C
(425°F), Gas Mark 7, for 30 minutes.

Heat the oil in a pan, add the
spring onions and fry until lightly
browned. Remove and set aside.

Remove the duck from the oven
and pour off any excess fat. Lower
oven temperature to 190°C (375°F),
Gas Mark 5. Sprinkle duck with the
spring onions, remaining marinade
and stock. Cover with foil. Return to the
oven for 1 hour, basting occasionally.

Place the duck on a board, joint
and chop into 16 pieces. Reassemble
on a warmed serving dish; keep hot.

Put the pineapple and juice in a
pan. Stir in the sherry, blended
cornflour and duck juices. Cook for
2 minutes and serve in a sauce bowl.

Garnish the duck with pineapple
and spring onions to serve.
Serves 4 to 6

Peking Duck

1 x 1.75-2 kg
(4-4 ½ lb)
oven-ready duck
2 tablespoons soy
sauce
2 tablespoons dark
brown sugar
MANDARIN
PANCAKES:
500 g (1 lb) plain
flour
pinch of salt
300 ml (½ pint)
boiling water
(approximately)
sesame seed oil*
TO SERVE:
1 small cucumber, cut
into 5 cm (2 inch)
matchstick pieces
1 bunch spring
onions, cut into
5 cm (2 inch)
matchstick pieces
8 tablespoons hoisin
sauce*
spring onion flower*

Immerse the duck in a pan of boiling water for 2 minutes, then drain thoroughly. Hang up the duck to dry in a well ventilated room overnight.

Mix the soy sauce and sugar together and rub over the duck. Hang for 2 hours until the coating is dry.

Place the duck on a rack in a roasting pan and cook in a preheated moderately hot oven, 200°C (400°F), Gas Mark 6, for 1½ hours.

Meanwhile, make the pancakes. Sift the flour and salt into a mixing bowl. Gradually add the boiling water, mixing to make a stiff dough. Knead and shape into a roll, 5 cm (2 inches) in diameter. Cut into 1 cm (½ inch) slices, then roll out into thin 15 cm (6 inch) diameter pancakes. Brush one side of each pancake with sesame seed oil and sandwich the pancakes together in pairs.

Place an ungreased frying pan over a high heat. When hot, lower the heat slightly and place a pancake 'sandwich' in the pan. When it starts to puff up, turn and cook the other side until lightly browned.

Pull the 2 pancakes apart and fold each in half. Place on a warmed serving dish and cover with foil to prevent them drying out; keep warm.

Cut off all the crispy skin from the duck and arrange on a warmed serving dish. Garnish with cucumber. Remove all the meat and arrange on another warmed serving dish. Garnish with spring onion. Place the hoisin sauce in a small bowl. Garnish the pancakes with a spring onion flower.

To eat, spread a little hoisin sauce over a pancake. Cover with a piece of duck skin and meat, then top with a few pieces of cucumber and spring onion. Roll up the pancake.
Serves 4 to 6

Duck with Almonds

500 g (1 lb) lean
  duck meat
2 slices root ginger*,
  shredded
1 clove garlic, crushed
3 tablespoons oil
3-4 dried Chinese
  mushrooms*
  (optional)
4 spring onions,
  sliced
125 g (4 oz) canned
  bamboo shoots*,
  drained and sliced
3 tablespoons soy
  sauce
2 tablespoons sherry
2 teaspoons cornflour
25 g (1 oz) flaked
  almonds, toasted

Cut the duck into small chunks and place in a bowl with the ginger and garlic. Pour over 1 tablespoon of the oil and leave to marinate for 30 minutes.

Soak the mushrooms in warm water for 15 minutes, if using. Squeeze dry, discard the hard stalks, then slice the mushroom caps.

Heat the remaining oil in a wok or deep frying pan, add the spring onions and stir-fry for 30 seconds. Add the duck and cook for 2 minutes. Add the mushrooms, bamboo shoots, soy sauce and sherry and cook for 2 minutes. Blend the cornflour with 1 tablespoon water and stir into the pan. Cook for 1 minute, stirring, until thickened.

Stir in the toasted almonds and serve immediately.
Serves 4 to 6

Nanking Spiced Duck

125 g (4 oz) coarse
  salt
3 teaspoons
  Szechuan
  peppercorns*
1 x 1.75-2 kg
  (4-4 1/2 lb)
  oven-ready duck
TO GARNISH:
chilli flowers*
cucumber twists and
  slices

Place the salt and peppercorns in a frying pan over high heat for 10 minutes to brown, taking care not to burn; cool.

Rub this mixture thoroughly over the inside and outside of the duck. Wrap lightly in foil and store in the refrigerator for 3 days.

Remove the foil and place the duck on a rack in a roasting pan. Cook in a preheated moderately hot oven, 200°C (400°F), Gas Mark 6, for 1 1/4 to 1 1/2 hours, until golden brown.

Transfer to a warmed serving dish and garnish with chilli flowers and cucumber. Serve immediately.
Serves 4 to 6

MEAT DISHES

Stir-Fried Shredded Beef with Ginger

500 g (1 lb) rump
   steak, shredded
1 teaspoon salt
2 tablespoons oil
2 cloves garlic, sliced
8 pieces root ginger*,
   shredded
4 tablespoons soy
   sauce
2 tablespoons dry
   sherry
4 spring onions,
   shredded
shredded root ginger*
   and spring onion
   to garnish

Sprinkle the steak with the salt. Heat the oil in a wok or deep frying pan, add the garlic and fry quickly until browned. Add the meat and ginger and stir-fry for 2 minutes. Stir in the soy sauce and sherry and cook for 1 minute. Stir in the spring onions.

Spoon onto a warmed serving dish and sprinkle with the ginger and spring onions. Serve immediately.
Serves 4 to 6

Red-Cooked Beef with Broccoli

1 kg (2 lb) lean
  stewing steak
1 piece root ginger*,
  finely chopped
2 cloves garlic,
  crushed
6 tablespoons soy
  sauce
3 tablespoons dry
  sherry
50 g (2 oz) sugar
  crystals
1 teaspoon 5-spice
  powder*
600 ml (1 pint) beef
  stock
500 g (1 lb) broccoli
TO GARNISH:
radish flower*
shredded spring onions

Cut the meat into 2.5 cm (1 inch) cubes and place in a saucepan. Add the ginger, garlic, soy sauce and sherry. Sprinkle over the sugar and 5-spice powder.

Pour in the stock and bring to the boil, then cover and simmer for 1 to 1½ hours, until the meat is tender.

Divide the broccoli into florets and add to the pan. Boil vigorously, uncovered, until the broccoli is just cooked and the stock reduced and thickened.

Arrange the meat and broccoli on a warmed serving dish and garnish with a radish flower and shredded spring onions. Serve immediately.
Serves 4 to 6

Quick-Fried Beef in Oyster Sauce

4 carrots
2 celery sticks
2 tablespoons oil
4 spring onions,
   chopped
2 cloves garlic, sliced
350 g (12 oz) rump
   or sirloin steak
salt
125 g (4 oz) bean
   sprouts*
1 tablespoon soy
   sauce
2 tablespoons dry
   sherry
3 tablespoons oyster
   sauce*
TO GARNISH:
carrot flower*
celery leaves

Slice the carrots and celery sticks
diagonally.

Heat the oil in a wok or frying
pan, add the spring onions and garlic
and fry quickly for about 30 seconds.
Add the carrots and celery and
stir-fry for 1 minute.

Cut the steak into thin slices and
sprinkle with salt. Add to the pan
and fry until browned on all sides.
Stir in the bean sprouts, soy sauce,
sherry and oyster sauce and cook for
2 minutes.

Spoon the mixture onto a warmed
serving dish and garnish with the
carrot flower and celery leaves to
serve.
Serves 4 to 6

Deep-Fried Beef Slices

4 spring onions,
    chopped
pinch of salt
1 tablespoon dry
    sherry
1 piece root ginger*,
    finely chopped
1 tablespoon chilli
    sauce
1 chilli, seeded and
    finely chopped
500 g (1 lb) rump
    steak
oil for deep-frying
BATTER:
4 tablespoons plain
    flour
pinch of salt
1 egg
3-4 tablespoons water
TO GARNISH:
coriander leaves*
lemon slice

Put the spring onions, salt, sherry,
ginger, chilli sauce and chilli in a
bowl and mix well. Cut the steak
into thin slices and add to the
marinade. Toss well to coat and
leave to marinate for 20 to 25
minutes.

Meanwhile, make the batter. Sift
the flour and salt into a bowl, break
in the egg and beat well, adding
sufficient water to make a smooth
batter.

Heat the oil in a wok or
deep-fryer. Dip the steak slices into
the batter and deep-fry in hot oil
until golden brown. Drain on
kitchen paper.

Arrange the meat on a warmed
serving dish and garnish with
coriander and a lemon slice. Serve
immediately, with soy sauce handed
separately.
Serves 4 to 6

Szechuan Hot Shredded Beef

500 g (1 lb) rump or
    frying steak
2 tablespoons
    cornflour
salt
3 tablespoons oil
4 spring onions,
    chopped
2 celery sticks, sliced
    diagonally
4 carrots, sliced
    diagonally
2 tablespoons soy
    sauce
1 tablespoon hoisin
    sauce*
3 teaspoons chilli
    sauce
2 tablespoons dry
    sherry
TO GARNISH:
carrot flowers*
celery leaves

Cut the steak into 5 cm (2 inch) long thin slices. Toss the steak in the cornflour and season with salt to taste.

Heat the oil in a wok or deep frying pan, add the spring onions and fry for 1 minute. Add the meat slices and cook for 4 minutes, stirring, until the meat is lightly browned. Add the celery and carrots and cook for 2 minutes. Stir in the soy, hoisin and chilli sauces and the sherry, bring to the boil and cook for 1 minute.

Arrange on a warmed serving dish, garnish with carrot flowers and celery leaves and serve immediately.
Serves 4 to 6

Casserole of Lion's Head

750 g (1½ lb) finely
   minced pork
1 teaspoon salt
2 cloves garlic, crushed
2 pieces root ginger*,
   finely chopped
4 tablespoons soy
   sauce
3 tablespoons dry
   sherry
4 spring onions,
   finely chopped
1 tablespoon
   cornflour
oil for deep-frying
300 ml (½ pint) beef
   stock
750 g (1½ lb)
   spinach
TO GARNISH:
chopped spring onion

Put the pork in a bowl, stir in the salt, garlic, ginger, 1 tablespoon each of the soy sauce and sherry, and 2 of the spring onions. Mix in the cornflour, then form the mixture into balls, the size of a walnut.

Heat the oil in a wok or deep-fryer, add the meat balls and deep-fry until golden brown. Drain on kitchen paper. Put the meat balls in a pan and add the remaining soy sauce, sherry and spring onions. Spoon over the stock, cover and simmer for 15 to 20 minutes.

Meanwhile, cook the spinach, with just the water clinging to the leaves after washing, for 5 to 10 minutes until tender. Transfer to a warmed serving dish, arrange the meat balls on top and garnish with spring onion. Serve immediately.
Serves 4 to 6

Sweet and Sour Pork with Chinese Cabbage

350 g (12 oz) lean
   pork, cubed
salt and pepper
2 tablespoons dry
   sherry
1 egg, beaten
1-2 tablespoons
   cornflour
oil for deep-frying
SAUCE:
1 tablespoon oil
4 spring onions,
   chopped
2 cloves garlic,
   crushed
1 piece root ginger*,
   finely chopped
1 green pepper,
   cored, seeded and
   finely chopped
4 tablespoons wine
   vinegar
2 tablespoons tomato
   purée
1 tablespoon soy
   sauce
3 tablespoons clear
   honey
1 tablespoon
   cornflour blended
   with 2 tablespoons
   cold water
2 tablespoons sesame
   seed oil*
TO SERVE:
1 small Chinese
   cabbage*, roughly
   chopped
green pepper rings
red chilli flower*

Put the pork in a bowl, sprinkle with salt and pepper and stir in the sherry. Leave to marinate for 20 minutes.

Stir in the beaten egg and cornflour and mix well to coat the meat. Heat the oil in a wok or deep-fryer. Add the pork and fry until browned on all sides. Drain on kitchen paper.

To make the sauce, heat the oil in a wok or frying pan, add the spring onions, garlic and ginger and stir-fry for 2 minutes. Stir in the remaining ingredients, bring to the boil and cook for 2 minutes.

Stir in the cooked pork and cook for 2 minutes.

To serve, arrange the Chinese cabbage on a warmed serving dish and pile the sweet and sour pork on top. Garnish with pepper rings and a chilli flower.
Serves 4 to 6

Braised Leg of Pork

1.5-1.75 kg (3-4 lb)
  leg of pork
salt
6 spring onions, each
  cut into 3 pieces
2 pieces root ginger*,
  chopped
150 ml (¼ pint) soy
  sauce
6 tablespoons dry
  sherry
50 g (2 oz) soft
  brown sugar
TO GARNISH:
radish flowers*
turnip flowers*
spring onions

Rub the pork with salt; do not score the skin. Put the spring onions and ginger in a large pan, pour over the soy sauce and sherry, then stir in the sugar. Put the pork in the pan, turning to coat with the soy sauce mixture. Bring to the boil, cover and simmer for 2 to 2½ hours, until very tender, turning occasionally.

Remove the pork from the pan and keep hot. Boil the sauce until well reduced and thickened; pour into a sauce bowl. Carve the meat into thick slices, arrange on a serving dish and garnish with radish flowers, turnip flowers and spring onions. Serve hot or cold, with the sauce.

Serves 6 to 8

Stir-Fried Pork and Mange-Tout

350 g (12 oz) lean
   pork, thinly sliced
2 tablespoons soy
   sauce
2 tablespoons dry
   sherry
4 dried Chinese
   mushrooms*
1 tablespoon oil
250 g (8 oz)
   mange-tout

Put the pork in a bowl with the soy
sauce and sherry. Mix well to coat,
then leave to marinate for 15 minutes.

Soak the dried mushrooms in
warm water for 15 minutes. Squeeze
dry and discard the hard stalks, then
slice the mushroom caps.

Heat the oil in a wok or frying
pan, add the meat and marinade.
Stir-fry for 2 minutes, then add the
mushrooms and cook for 1 minute.
Add the mange-tout and stir-fry for
2 minutes.

Spoon the mixture onto a warmed
serving dish and serve immediately.
Serves 4 to 6

Sweet and Sour Spare Ribs

1 kg (2 lb) lean
   spare ribs
salt
2 tablespoons oil
1 piece root ginger*,
   finely chopped
1 clove garlic, crushed
SAUCE:
4 tablespoons clear
   honey
4 tablespoons malt
   vinegar
2 tablespoons soy
   sauce
1 x 142 g (5 oz) can
   tomato purée
1 teaspoon mixed
   herbs
2 teaspoons chilli
   powder
dash of Worcester-
   shire sauce
2 cloves garlic, crushed
TO GARNISH:
spring onion flowers*
tomato flower*

Mix all the sauce ingredients
together, cover and set aside.

Cut the spare ribs into 5 cm
(2 inch) pieces and sprinkle with salt.
Heat the oil in a wok or deep frying
pan, add the ginger and garlic and
fry for 1 minute. Add the spare ribs
and fry quickly until browned.
Lower the heat and cook for 10
minutes.

Spoon the sauce over the spare ribs
and turn to coat them evenly. Cover
the pan with foil or a lid and simmer
gently for 25 to 30 minutes, until the
meat is tender, stirring occasionally.

Arrange the spare ribs on a
warmed serving dish and garnish
with the spring onions and tomato
flower. Serve immediately.
Serves 4 to 6

Fried Wonton with Sweet and Sour Sauce

500 g (1 lb) wonton
  skins*
3 tablespoons soy
  sauce
1 tablespoon dry
  sherry
500 g (1 lb) minced
  pork
1 teaspoon brown
  sugar
1 clove garlic,
  crushed
1 piece root ginger*,
  finely chopped
250 g (8 oz) frozen
  spinach, thawed
  and squeezed dry
oil for deep-frying
SAUCE:
1 tablespoon oil
2 cloves garlic,
  crushed
2 tablespoons soy
  sauce
2 tablespoons clear
  honey
2 tablespoons wine
  vinegar
2 teaspoons chilli
  sauce
1 tablespoon dry
  sherry
2 tablespoons tomato
  purée
2 teaspoons
  cornflour, blended
  with 1 tablespoon
  water
TO GARNISH:
spring onion flowers*

Cut out 5 cm (2 inch) squares from
the wonton skins. Put the soy sauce,
sherry and pork in a bowl and mix
well. Add the sugar, garlic, ginger
and spinach and mix well. Spoon a
little of this mixture onto the centre
of each wonton skin. Dampen the
edges and fold to form triangles,
pressing the edges together firmly to
ensure that the filling does not come
out during frying.

Heat the oil in a wok or deep-fryer
and fry the wonton, a few at a time,
for about 5 minutes until golden
brown. Drain on kitchen paper and
keep hot.

To make the sauce, heat the oil in
a pan, add the garlic and fry for
1 minute. Stir in the remaining
ingredients, bring to the boil and
simmer for 2 minutes. Spoon into a
small serving bowl.

Arrange the wonton on a warmed
serving dish, with the sauce bowl in
the centre. Garnish with spring
onion flowers. Serve immediately,
dipping each wonton into the sauce
before eating.
Serves 4 to 6

Braised Pork with Pumpkin

350 g (12 oz) lean
   pork
4 tablespoons soy
   sauce
3 tablespoons dry
   sherry
500 g (1 lb) pumpkin
4 spring onions
2 tablespoons oil
1 piece root ginger*,
   shredded
2 cloves garlic, sliced
TO GARNISH:
carrot flowers*
spring onion slices
coriander leaves*

Cut the pork into 1 cm (½ inch)
slices. Put the soy sauce and sherry in
a bowl and add the pork. Mix well
and leave to marinate for 20 minutes.

Cut the pumpkin into 2.5 cm
(1 inch) cubes. Slice each spring
onion into 3 pieces. Heat the oil in a
wok or frying pan, add the pumpkin
and fry quickly until browned. Add
the spring onions, ginger and garlic
and cook for 1 minute. Add the pork
and marinade and cook for 12 to 15
minutes, until the pork and pumpkin
are tender.

Spoon the mixture onto a warmed
serving dish, garnish with carrot
flowers, spring onion slices and
coriander. Serve immediately.
Serves 4 to 6

Crispy Barbecued Pork

1.5 kg (3 lb) lean
  belly pork, in one
  piece
salt
1 tablespoon soy
  sauce
1 teaspoon 5-spice
  powder*
TO GARNISH:
radish rose*
turnip flowers*
coriander leaves*

Pour a kettleful of boiling water over
the skin of the pork; drain and dry.
Rub all the surfaces of the meat with
salt and leave to dry for 45 minutes.

Using a very sharp knife, score the
skin of the pork in a diamond
pattern. Pierce the meat with a
skewer in several places. Rub the soy
sauce and 5-spice powder into the
pork. Cover and leave for 1 hour.

Place the pork, skin side up, in a
roasting pan and cook in a preheated
hot oven, 230°C (450°F), Gas Mark
8, for 20 minutes. Lower the
temperature to 200°C (400°F), Gas
Mark 6, and cook for a further 50 to
55 minutes, or until the pork is
tender and the skin is very crisp.

Arrange the meat on a warmed
serving dish and garnish with the
radish rose, turnip flowers and
coriander. Cut into slices to serve.
Serves 6 to 8

Red-Cooked Lamb

1 kg (2 lb) lean
  lamb, cubed
4 cloves garlic, sliced
3 pieces root ginger*,
  finely chopped
1 teaspoon 5-spice
  powder*
6 tablespoons soy
  sauce
3 tablespoons dry
  sherry
6 spring onions
600 ml (1 pint) beef
  stock
50 g (2 oz) soft
  brown sugar
1 red pepper and
  1 green pepper,
  cored, seeded and
  diced

Put the lamb in a saucepan, sprinkle
with the garlic and ginger and mix
well. Add the 5-spice powder, soy
sauce and sherry.

Cut each spring onion into 3
pieces and sprinkle over the lamb.
Pour over the stock and stir in the
brown sugar. Bring to the boil,
cover and simmer for 1 to 1¼ hours,
until the meat is tender. Remove the
lid and increase the heat to reduce the
remaining stock to a thick sauce.

Spoon the red-cooked lamb and
sauce onto a warmed serving dish.
Sprinkle with the red and green
peppers and serve immediately.
Serves 4 to 6

Stir-Fried Lamb with Noodles

125 g (4 oz)
    transparent
    noodles*
500 g (1 lb) very
    lean lamb
1 tablespoon oil
3 spring onions
1 piece root ginger*
2 cloves garlic, sliced
2 celery sticks,
    chopped
1 red pepper, cored,
    seeded and sliced
2 tablespoons light
    soy sauce*
2 tablespoons dry
    sherry
150 ml (¼ pint)
    stock
2 teaspoons sesame
    seed oil*

TO GARNISH:
green chilli flowers*
spring onion flowers*

Soak the noodles in warm water for
10 minutes; drain. Cut the lamb into
thin slices. Finely chop the spring
onions and ginger.

Heat the oil in a wok or frying
pan, add the spring onions, ginger
and garlic and stir-fry for 1 minute.
Add the celery and lamb and cook
for 2 minutes. Add the red pepper,
soy sauce and sherry and bring to the
boil. Stir in the stock and noodles
and simmer for 5 minutes. Sprinkle
with the sesame seed oil.

Transfer to a warmed serving dish
and garnish with chilli and spring
onion flowers. Serve immediately.
Serves 4 to 6

Tung-Po Lamb

750 g (1½ lb) very
   lean lamb
4 spring onions
250 g (8 oz) carrots
4 celery sticks
2 tablespoons oil
3 tablespoons soy
   sauce
4 tablespoons dry
   sherry
2 leeks, sliced
4 cloves garlic, thinly
   sliced
2 pieces root ginger*,
   shredded
1 teaspoon lightly
   crushed black
   peppercorns
2 teaspoons sugar
TO GARNISH:
lemon slices
coriander leaves*

Cut the lamb into thin slices. Cut
each spring onion into 3 pieces. Slice
the carrots and celery diagonally.

Heat the oil in a wok or deep
frying pan, add the lamb and brown
on both sides. Lower the heat, add
the carrots and celery and stir-fry for
2 minutes. Stir in the soy sauce and
sherry. Cover and cook for 15
minutes, until the vegetables are
tender.

Add the leeks, garlic, spring
onions and ginger and cook for
1 minute. Add the peppercorns and
sugar and heat through until the
sugar dissolves.

Spoon the Tung-Po onto a
warmed serving dish, garnish with
lemon and coriander and serve
immediately.
Serves 4 to 6

Mongolian Lamb Hot Pot

1 kg (2 lb) piece
  frozen lamb fillet
50 g (2 oz)
  transparent
  noodles*
1 large Chinese
  cabbage*
500 g (1 lb) spinach
2 cakes bean curd*,
  thinly sliced
3 x 411 g (14½ oz)
  cans consommé
SAUCES:
6 spring onions,
  chopped
2 tablespoons
  shredded root
  ginger*
6 tablespoons sesame
  seed paste*
3 tablespoons sesame
  seed oil*
6 tablespoons soy
  sauce
4 tablespoons chilli
  sauce
4 tablespoons
  chopped coriander*
  (optional)

Allow the lamb to defrost slightly, but while it is still partially frozen, cut into paper-thin slices, arrange on a serving dish and allow to thaw.

Soak the noodles in hot water for 10 minutes; drain thoroughly.

Place the cabbage leaves and spinach in a basket or dish. Arrange the bean curd and noodles on another dish.

Combine the spring onions and ginger in a sauce dish. Mix the sesame seed paste and oil in another sauce bowl. Put the soy sauce and chilli sauce in individual sauce bowls. If liked, serve chopped coriander in a separate bowl.

Heat the consommé in a fondue pot or similar dish at the table.

To serve, each diner first mixes his own sauce in a small dish. Using chopsticks, fondue forks or long skewers, each person dips a slice of meat into the hot consommé to cook, then dips it into his prepared sauce before eating.

When all the meat has been eaten the vegetables, bean curd and noodles are added to the pot and cooked for about 5 to 10 minutes. Serve this soup at the end of the meal.
Serves 4 to 6

Stir-Fried Kidney Flowers

15 g (¼ oz) wooden
  ears* (optional)
500 g (1 lb) pigs'
  kidney
4 tablespoons oil
75 g (3 oz) canned
  bamboo shoots*,
  drained and sliced
75 g (3 oz) canned
  water chestnuts*,
  drained and sliced
2 celery sticks, sliced
  diagonally
4 spring onions,
  sliced
2 cloves garlic, sliced
1 piece root ginger*,
  finely chopped
125 g (4 oz) frozen
  spinach, thawed
3 tablespoons soy
  sauce
1 tablespoon wine
  vinegar

Soak the wooden ears in warm water for 10 minutes, if using; drain.

Remove the thin white film and any fat from the kidneys, cut each one in half lengthways and discard the white core. Score the surface of each kidney in a diagonal criss-cross pattern, then cut into 2 or 3 pieces.

Heat the oil in a wok or deep frying pan, add the kidney and fry for 1 minute, stirring constantly; the kidneys will curl up to form little flowers. Remove from the pan and keep warm. Add the wooden ears, if using, bamboo shoots, water chestnuts, celery, spring onions, garlic and ginger and stir-fry for 2 minutes.

Return the kidney flowers to the pan with the spinach. Stir in the soy sauce and vinegar and cook for 1 to 2 minutes. Spoon onto a warmed serving dish and serve immediately.
Serves 4 to 6

Fried Liver, Szechuan-Style

500 g (1 lb) lambs'
  liver, sliced
salt and pepper
2 tablespoons dry
  sherry
2 tablespoons oil
50 g (2 oz) canned
  bamboo shoots*,
  drained and sliced
3 spring onions,
  chopped
1 clove garlic, crushed
¼ cauliflower
2 carrots
2 tablespoons
  Szechuan pickled
  vegetables*
2 tablespoons soy
  sauce

Season the liver with salt and pepper to taste. Mix in the sherry and leave to marinate for 15 minutes.

Heat the oil in a wok or deep frying pan, add the bamboo shoots, spring onions and garlic and stir-fry for 1 minute.

Divide the cauliflower into florets and slice the carrots diagonally. Add both to the pan and cook, stirring, for 2 minutes. Add the liver and sherry and fry quickly until browned all over. Stir in the Szechuan vegetables and soy sauce and bring to the boil. Spoon onto a warmed serving dish and serve immediately.
Serves 4 to 6

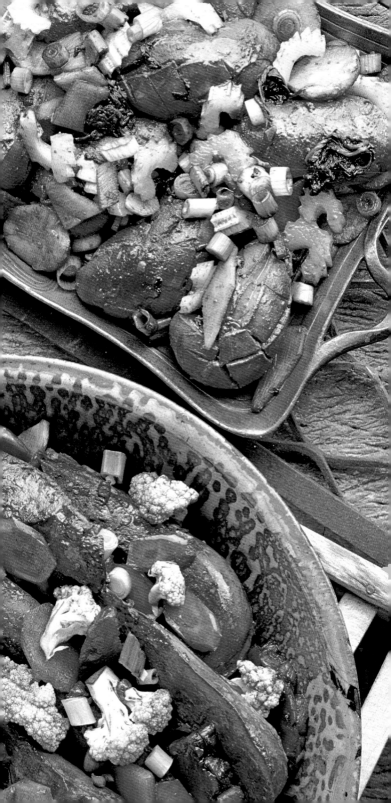

Omelet with Meat Sauce

3 tablespoons oil
1 clove garlic, crushed
2 spring onions,
    finely chopped
2 celery sticks,
    chopped
1 boned chicken
    breast, diced
125 g (4 oz) minced
    pork
2 teaspoons cornflour
1 tablespoon dry
    sherry
2 tablespoons soy
    sauce
OMELET:
6 eggs, beaten
salt and pepper
TO GARNISH:
spring onion flowers*
celery leaves

Heat 1 tablespoon of the oil in a wok or frying pan, add the garlic, spring onions and celery and cook for 1 minute. Increase the heat, add the chicken and pork and cook for 2 minutes.

Blend the cornflour with 1 tablespoon water. Stir into the sauce with the sherry and soy sauce and simmer, stirring occasionally, for 15 minutes.

Meanwhile, make the omelet. Season the eggs with salt and pepper to taste. Heat the remaining 2 tablespoons oil in a large frying pan, pour in the eggs and cook gently, drawing the cooked edges towards the centre with a fork, until set and browned on both sides.

Carefully transfer to a warmed serving dish. Spoon over the meat sauce and garnish with spring onions and celery leaves. Serve immediately.
Serves 4 to 6

Crispy Spring Rolls

250 g (8 oz) plain flour
pinch of salt
1 egg
300 ml (½ pint) water (approximately)
oil for deep-frying
FILLING:
1 tablespoon oil
250 g (8 oz) lean pork, shredded
1 clove garlic, crushed
2 celery sticks, sliced
125 g (4 oz) button mushrooms, sliced
2 spring onions, chopped
125 g (4 oz) bean sprouts*
125 g (4 oz) frozen peeled prawns, thawed
2 tablespoons soy sauce

Sift the flour and salt into a bowl. Add the egg and beat in sufficient water to make a smooth batter.

Lightly oil a 20 cm (8 inch) frying pan and place over moderate heat. Pour in just enough batter to cover the base of the pan. Cook until the underside is pale brown, then turn and cook the other side. Remove from the pan and put on one side. Repeat with the remaining batter.

To make the filling: Heat the oil in a pan, add the pork and brown quickly. Add the garlic and vegetables; stir-fry for 2 minutes. Mix in the prawns and soy sauce. Leave until cool.

Place 2 to 3 tablespoons of the filling in the centre of each pancake. Fold in the sides and form into a tight roll, sticking down the edge with a little flour and water paste.

Heat the oil in a wok or deep-fryer and deep-fry the spring rolls a few at a time until golden brown. Drain on kitchen paper. Serve immediately.
Serves 4 to 6

RICE, NOODLES & DUMPLINGS

Vegetable Rice

2 tablespoons oil
2 leeks, sliced
1 piece root ginger*,
   finely chopped
1 clove garlic, sliced
250 g (8 oz) long-
   grain rice
salt
250 g (8 oz) spring
   greens, shredded

Heat the oil in a wok or deep frying pan, add the leeks, ginger and garlic and fry quickly for 30 seconds. Add the rice, stirring to coat each grain with the oil mixture. Add sufficient boiling water just to cover the rice. Season to taste with salt. Bring to the boil, cover and simmer for 5 minutes. Add the greens, bring back to the boil and simmer for 7 to 9 minutes until the rice is just tender.

Drain and serve immediately.

Serves 4 to 6

Fried Rice

3 tablespoons oil
3 spring onions, chopped
125 g (4 oz) button mushrooms, sliced
3 eggs, beaten
50 g (2 oz) cooked lean ham, diced
50 g (2 oz) frozen peeled prawns, thawed
175 g (6 oz) long-grain rice, cooked
1 tablespoon soy sauce
50 g (2 oz) frozen peas

Heat the oil in a wok or frying pan, add the spring onions and mushrooms and cook for 30 seconds. Add the eggs and scramble lightly over a low heat. Transfer to a warmed plate and set aside.

Add the remaining ingredients and stir-fry for 2 minutes. Return the scrambled egg mixture to the pan and cook for 1 minute.

Pile onto a warmed serving dish and serve immediately.
Serves 4

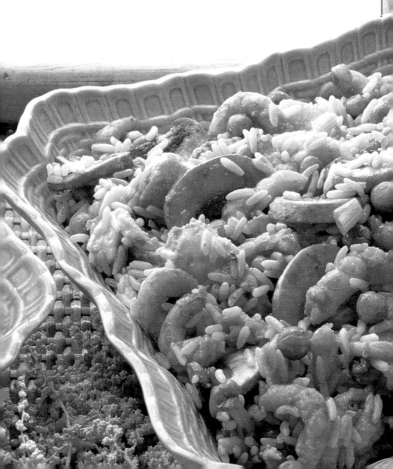

Lotus Leaf Rice

8 lotus leaves*
1 tablespoon oil
1 clove garlic, crushed
3 spring onions,
  chopped
125 g (4 oz) button
  mushrooms, sliced
50 g (2 oz) cooked
  ham, diced
125 g (4 oz) cooked
  chicken, diced
few green peas
50 g (2 oz) canned
  bamboo shoots*,
  drained and
  chopped
175 g (6 oz) long-
  grain rice, cooked
2 tablespoons soy
  sauce
2 tablespoons dry
  sherry

Soak the lotus leaves in warm water for 30 minutes. Drain thoroughly.

Heat the oil in a wok or deep frying pan, add the garlic and spring onions and stir-fry for 1 minute. Add the remaining ingredients, except the lotus leaves, and cook for 2 minutes.

Cut each lotus leaf into 2 or 3 pieces and divide the mixture between them, spooning into the centre. Fold the leaf, enclosing the filling, to form a parcel and secure with string or raffia. Place in a steamer and steam vigorously for 15 to 20 minutes.

Pile the parcels onto a warmed serving dish and serve immediately; each diner opens his own parcels.

Serves 4 to 6

NOTE: If lotus leaves are unavailable use vine leaves instead. You will need one vine leaf for each parcel.

Dan-Dan Noodles

500 g (1 lb) noodles
salt
2 tablespoons sesame
  seed paste*
6 spring onions,
  chopped
2 cloves garlic, crushed
1 piece root ginger*,
  finely chopped
1 tablespoon soy
  sauce
2 teaspoons red wine
  vinegar
900 ml (1½ pints)
  beef or chicken
  stock
2 teaspoons hot
  pepper oil*
  (optional)

Cook the noodles in boiling salted water according to packet instructions, until just tender. Drain and keep hot.

Blend the sesame seed paste with 4 tablespoons water and place in a pan, together with the remaining ingredients, except the stock and pepper oil. Cook over moderate heat, stirring frequently, for about 5 minutes.

Meanwhile, bring the stock to the boil and simmer for 2 minutes.

Divide the noodles and hot sauce between 4 individual soup bowls. Spoon over the hot stock and top with the hot pepper oil, if using. Serve immediately.

Serves 4

Mixed Seafood Stick Noodles

4 dried Chinese
  mushrooms*
500 g (1 lb) rice stick
  noodles*
salt
2 tablespoons oil
4 spring onions,
  chopped
2 cloves garlic, sliced
1 piece root ginger*,
  finely chopped
50 g (2 oz) frozen
  peeled prawns,
  thawed
125 g (4 oz) fresh or
  frozen squid,
  sliced (optional)
1 x 225 g (7.5 oz)
  can clams, drained
2 tablespoons dry
  sherry
1 tablespoon soy
  sauce

Soak the mushrooms in warm water
for 15 minutes. Squeeze well, discard
the stalks, then slice the mushroom
caps.

Cook the rice stick noodles in
boiling salted water for 7 to 8
minutes until just tender. Drain and
rinse in cold water. Keep on one
side.

Heat the oil in a wok or deep
frying pan, add the spring onions,
garlic and ginger and stir-fry for
30 seconds. Stir in the mushrooms,
prawns and squid, if using, then
cook for 2 minutes. Stir in the
remaining ingredients, then carefully
stir in the noodles and heat through.

Pile the mixture into a warmed
serving dish and serve immediately.
Serves 4 to 6

Noodles Tossed with Meat and Vegetables

2 carrots
3 celery sticks
1/2 cucumber
2 green chillies,
    seeded
2 tablespoons oil
1 clove garlic
350 g (12 oz)
    minced pork
4 spring onions,
    sliced
1 small green pepper,
    cored, seeded and
    sliced
1 tablespoon soy
    sauce
2 tablespoons sweet
    red bean paste*
1 tablespoon dry
    sherry
350 g (12 oz)
    noodles, cooked

Cut the carrots, celery and cucumber into matchstick lengths. Slice the chillies and garlic thinly.

Heat the oil in a wok or deep frying pan, add the chillies and garlic and fry quickly for about 30 seconds. Add the pork and cook for 2 minutes. Increase the heat, add the vegetables and cook for 1 minute. Stir in the soy sauce, bean paste, sherry and noodles. Stir well to mix and heat through.

Pile onto a warmed serving dish and serve immediately.

Serves 4 to 6

Crispy Fried Noodles

3 celery sticks
125 g (4 oz) spinach
500 g (1 lb) egg
    noodles
salt
1 tablespoon oil
1 clove garlic, sliced
1 piece root ginger*,
    finely chopped
3 spring onions,
    chopped
125 g (4 oz) lean
    pork, sliced
125 g (4 oz) boned
    chicken breast,
    shredded
1 tablespoon soy
    sauce
1 tablespoon dry
    sherry
50 g (2 oz) frozen
    peeled prawns,
    thawed

Slice the celery sticks diagonally and shred the spinach.

Cook the noodles in boiling salted water according to the packet instructions until just tender; do not overcook. Drain and rinse with cold water.

Heat the oil in a wok or deep frying pan, add the garlic, ginger and spring onions and fry for 1 minute. Add the pork and chicken and stir-fry for 2 minutes. Add the noodles and remaining ingredients and cook for 3 minutes.

Pile onto a warmed serving dish and serve immediately.

Serves 4 to 6

Fried Steamed Dumplings

500 g (1 lb) self-
   raising flour
pinch of salt
200-250 ml (1/3 pint-
   8 fl oz) water
oil for deep-frying
FILLING:
350 g (12 oz)
   minced pork
1 tablespoon each
   soy sauce and
   dry sherry
2 teaspoons sesame
   seed oil*
2 spring onions,
   finely chopped
1 piece root ginger*,
   finely chopped
125 g (4 oz) canned
   bamboo shoots*,
   drained and
   chopped
TO GARNISH:
radish flowers*
spring onions

Sift the flour and salt into a mixing bowl. Add sufficient water to mix to a firm dough. Divide in half and knead each piece on a floured surface. Form each piece into a roll, 5 cm (2 inches) in diameter. Slice both rolls into 14 equal pieces. Roll out each piece into a 7.5 cm (3 inch) circle.

Mix all the filling ingredients together and divide the filling evenly between the rounds, placing it in the centre. Gather the sides of the dough up around the filling to meet at the top, then firmly twist the top of the dough to close tightly.

Arrange the dumplings on a moist piece of muslin in a steamer and steam vigorously for 20 minutes; drain.

Heat the oil in a wok or deep-fryer, add the dumplings and fry for 5 to 6 minutes until golden brown all over. Drain on kitchen paper.

Serve immediately, garnished with radish flowers and spring onions.
Serves 4 to 6

VEGETABLE DISHES

Braised White Cabbage

1 large Chinese
    cabbage*
250 g (8 oz) spinach
125 g (4 oz) spring
    greens
2 tablespoons oil
4 spring onions,
    chopped
1 tablespoon light
    soy sauce*
2 teaspoons dry
    sherry
50 g (2 oz) frozen
    peeled prawns,
    thawed

Cut the cabbage into 5 cm (2 inch) slices. Chop the spinach and greens.

Heat the oil in a wok or deep frying pan, add the spring onions and stir-fry for 1 minute. Add the cabbage, spinach and greens and stir over a medium heat for 2 minutes. Pour over the soy sauce and sherry and cook for 2 minutes. Add the prawns and cook for 1 minute.

Spoon into a warmed serving dish and serve immediately.

Serves 4 to 6

Fried Lettuce and Prawns

3 tablespoons oil
3 spring onions, cut
    into 2.5 cm
    (1 inch) lengths
1 piece root ginger*,
    shredded
125 g (4 oz) frozen
    peeled prawns,
    thawed
1 large or 2 medium
    Cos lettuce
1 tablespoon dry
    sherry
salt

Heat the oil in a wok or deep frying pan, add the spring onions and stir-fry for 30 seconds until lightly browned. Add the ginger and prawns and cook for 1 minute. Separate the lettuce into leaves and add to the pan with the sherry and salt to taste. Stir quickly for 1 to 2 minutes until the lettuce leaves are just limp.

Arrange on a warmed serving dish and serve immediately.

Serves 4 to 6

Steamed Stuffed Aubergines

1 tablespoon oil
2 cloves garlic, crushed
1 piece root ginger*,
    finely chopped
4 spring onions,
    chopped
2 red or green
    chillies, seeded and
    chopped
250 g (8 oz) minced
    pork
2 tablespoons soy
    sauce
2 tablespoons dry
    sherry
4 medium aubergines
50 g (2 oz) frozen
    peeled prawns,
    thawed
TO GARNISH:
spring onion flowers*

Heat the oil in a wok or deep frying pan, add the garlic, ginger and spring onions and stir-fry for 1 minute. Increase the heat, add the chillies and pork and cook for 2 minutes. Stir in the soy sauce and sherry and cook for 10 minutes.

Meanwhile, cut the aubergines in half lengthways, carefully scoop out the flesh and chop finely. Reserve the shells. Add the flesh to the pan and cook for 10 minutes. Stir in the prawns and cook for 1 minute.

Bring a large pan of water to the boil, add the aubergine shells and cook for 1 minute; remove from the pan and drain well. Spoon the stuffing mixture into the shells and place in an ovenproof dish. Cover with a lid or foil, place in a steamer and steam vigorously for 25 to 30 minutes.

Arrange on a warmed serving dish, garnish with spring onion flowers and serve immediately.
Serves 4 to 6

Stir-Fried Summer Vegetables

2 tablespoons oil
2 spring onions,
    sliced
1 piece root ginger*,
    sliced
2 cloves garlic, sliced
2 chillies, seeded and
    chopped
50 g (2 oz) button
    mushrooms
125 g (4 oz) baby
    carrots
125 g (4 oz)
    mange-tout
125 g (4 oz) French
    beans
50 g (2 oz) bean
    sprouts*
1 red pepper, cored
    seeded and sliced
2 celery sticks, sliced
few cauliflower florets
4 tablespoons light
    soy sauce*
2 tablespoons dry
    sherry
1 teaspoon sesame
    seed oil*

Heat the oil in a wok or deep frying pan, add the spring onions, ginger and garlic and stir-fry for about 30 seconds. Add the chillies and all the vegetables. Toss well and cook, stirring, for 2 minutes. Stir in the soy sauce and sherry and cook for 2 minutes.

Sprinkle over the sesame seed oil, pile into a warmed serving dish and serve immediately.

Serves 4 to 6

Dry-Cooked Bamboo Shoots

2 tablespoons dried
  shrimps*
  (optional)
2 tablespoons oil
1 x 500 g (1 lb) can
  bamboo shoots*,
  drained
1 piece root ginger*,
  finely chopped
50 g (2 oz)
  Szechuan pickled
  vegetables*,
  chopped
2 teaspoons caster
  sugar
pinch of salt
150 ml (¼ pint)
  chicken stock
2 red peppers, cored,
  seeded and sliced
1 tablespoon sesame
  seed oil*

Soak the dried shrimps in warm
water for 15 minutes, if using; drain.

Heat the oil in a wok or deep
frying pan, add the bamboo shoots
and stir-fry for 2 minutes until pale
brown around the edges. Remove
from the pan and drain on kitchen
paper.

Add the ginger, shrimps, if using,
and Szechuan pickles to the pan and
cook for 1 minute. Stir in the sugar,
salt and stock and bring to the boil.
Return the bamboo shoots to the
pan. Add the red peppers, mixing
well, and cook for 2 minutes.

Transfer to a warmed serving dish
and sprinkle over the sesame seed oil.
Serve immediately.
Serves 4 to 6

Bean Curd Fry

4 cakes bean curd*
4 tablespoons oil
1 clove garlic, sliced
2 small leeks, sliced
  diagonally
2 celery sticks, sliced
  diagonally
125 g (4 oz) button
  mushrooms, sliced
125 g (4 oz) lean
  pork, shredded
4 dried chillies,
  crushed
1 tablespoon chilli
  paste
1 tablespoon dry
  sherry

Cut each bean curd into 3 thin slices,
then cut each slice into 2 triangles.

Heat half the oil in a wok or deep
frying pan, add the garlic, leeks and
celery and fry quickly for 1 minute.
Stir in the mushrooms and pork and
cook for 2 minutes. Remove from
the pan and keep warm.

Heat the remaining oil in the pan,
add the bean curd and fry for 2
minutes; drain on kitchen paper.

Return the vegetables, pork and
bean curd to the pan, stir in the dried
chillies, chilli paste and sherry and
cook for 1 minute.

Transfer to a warmed serving dish,
discard the dried chillies and serve
immediately.
Serves 4 to 6

Chinese Cabbage and Mushrooms

8 dried Chinese
    mushrooms*
500 g (1 lb) Chinese
    cabbage leaves*
1 tablespoon oil
1 piece root ginger*,
    shredded
1 clove garlic, sliced
3 chillies, seeded and
    sliced
1 green pepper, cored,
    seeded and sliced
1 tablespoon each
    wine vinegar and
    light soy sauce*
1 teaspoon sesame
    seed oil*

Soak the mushrooms in warm water
for 15 minutes. Squeeze dry and
remove the hard stalks. Tear the
cabbage leaves into pieces.

Heat the oil in a wok or deep
frying pan, add the ginger, garlic and
chillies and stir-fry for 1 minute. Stir
in the green pepper, mushroom caps
and cabbage and cook for 1 minute.
Add the vinegar and soy sauce and
mix well.

Pile into a warmed serving dish
and sprinkle over the sesame seed oil.
Serve immediately.
Serves 4 to 6

Baked Stuffed Tomatoes

3 dried Chinese
   mushrooms*
1 tablespoon oil
1 large onion, finely
   chopped
500 g (1 lb) minced
   beef or pork
50 g (2 oz) canned
   water chestnuts*,
   drained and
   chopped
2 tablespoons soy
   sauce
2 tablespoons dry
   sherry
8 large tomatoes
1 tablespoon
   cornflour, blended
   with 2 tablespoons
   water
coriander leaves* to
   garnish

Soak the mushrooms in warm water for 15 minutes. Squeeze dry, discard the hard stalks and chop the caps.

Heat the oil in a wok or deep frying pan, add the onion and fry until browned. Add the meat and cook, stirring, for 5 minutes until evenly browned. Stir in the mushrooms, water chestnuts, soy sauce and sherry and cook for 2 minutes.

Cut the tomatoes in half, scoop out the flesh and add to the pan, discarding the seeds. Stir in the blended cornflour and cook, stirring, for 1 minute.

Cool slightly, then spoon the mixture into the tomato halves. Arrange in a baking dish and cook in a preheated moderate oven, 180°C (350°F), Gas Mark 4, for 15 to 25 minutes, until tender.

Serve hot, garnished with coriander.
Serves 4 to 8

Stuffed Green Peppers

1 tablespoon oil
1 clove garlic, crushed
1 piece root ginger*,
    finely chopped
250 g (8 oz) minced
    pork
1 spring onion,
    chopped
1 celery stick, finely
    chopped
grated rind of
    1 lemon
4 green peppers

Heat the oil in a wok or frying pan, add the garlic and fry until lightly browned. Lower the heat, add the ginger and pork and cook for 2 minutes. Stir in the spring onion, celery and lemon rind, mix well and cook for 30 seconds. Cool slightly.

Cut the peppers into quarters and remove the core and seeds. Divide the mixture between the pepper quarters, pressing it well into the cavity.

Arrange the pepper quarters in an oiled ovenproof dish. Cook in a preheated moderately hot oven, 200°C (400°F), Gas Mark 6, for 20 to 25 minutes, until tender. Transfer to a warmed serving dish and serve immediately.

Serves 4 to 6

Mushrooms in Oyster Sauce

50 g (2 oz) small
    dried Chinese
    mushrooms*
2 tablespoons oil
4 spring onions,
    chopped
150 ml (¼ pint)
    stock
1 x 227 g (8 oz) can
    straw mushrooms*,
    drained
125 g (4 oz) button
    mushrooms
3 tablespoons oyster
    sauce*
1 tablespoon dry
    sherry

Soak the dried mushrooms in warm water for 15 minutes. Drain, squeeze dry and discard the hard stalks.

Heat the oil in a wok or frying pan, add the spring onions and stir-fry for 30 seconds. Add the mushroom caps and pour over the stock. Simmer for 15 to 20 minutes, until the mushrooms are tender.

Add the straw mushrooms and button mushrooms and cook for 1 minute. Pour over the oyster sauce and sherry, stir well and cook for 2 minutes.

Pile into a warmed serving dish and serve immediately.
Serves 4 to 6

Quick-Braised Double Winter

10 dried Chinese
    mushrooms*
4 spring onions
2 tablespoons oil
175 g (6 oz) canned
    bamboo shoots*,
    drained and sliced
75 g (3 oz) canned
    water chestnuts*,
    drained and halved
2 tablespoons light
    soy sauce
1 tablespoon dry
    sherry
2 tablespoons stock
2 teaspoons cornflour
1 teaspoon sesame
    seed oil*

Soak the mushrooms in warm water for 15 minutes. Squeeze dry, discard the hard stalks and cut the mushroom caps into quarters. Cut the spring onions into 2.5 cm (1 inch) pieces.

Heat the oil in a wok or frying pan, add the spring onions, bamboo shoots and water chestnuts and stir-fry for 30 seconds. Add the mushrooms, stir in the soy sauce, sherry and stock and cook for 1 minute.

Blend the cornflour with 1 tablespoon water and stir into the pan. Cook, stirring, until thickened.

Spoon into a warmed serving dish, sprinkle with the sesame seed oil and serve immediately.
Serves 4 to 6

Bean Curd and Mushrooms

2 tablespoons oil
125 g (4 oz) lean
  pork, diced
4 spring onions,
  chopped
2 cloves garlic, sliced
1 green pepper, cored,
  seeded and diced
1 small cauliflower,
  broken into florets
125 g (4 oz) small
  flat mushrooms
1 tablespoon dry
  sherry
3 tablespoons crushed
  yellow bean
  sauce*
4 cakes bean curd*,
  diced

Heat the oil in a wok or deep frying
pan, add the pork, spring onions and
garlic and stir-fry for 2 minutes. Add
the green pepper, cauliflower and
mushrooms and cook for 1 minute.
Stir in the sherry and yellow bean
sauce and cook for 2 minutes. Stir in
the bean curd and cook for a further
minute.

Spoon into a warmed serving dish
and serve immediately.
Serves 4 to 6

Braised Aubergines

oil for shallow-frying
4 spring onions,
    sliced
4 cloves garlic, sliced
1 piece root ginger*,
    shredded
2 large aubergines,
    cut into 5 cm
    (2 inch) long
    strips
2 tablespoons soy
    sauce
2 tablespoons dry
    sherry
2 teaspoons chilli
    sauce
chopped red and
    green chillies to
    garnish

Heat 2 tablespoons oil in a wok or
deep frying pan. Add the spring
onions, garlic and ginger and stir-fry
for about 30 seconds. Remove from
the pan and set aside. Increase the
heat, add the aubergine strips and fry
until browned, adding more oil to
the pan as necessary. Remove from
the pan and drain on kitchen paper.

Pour off the oil from the pan.
Return the spring onions, garlic,
ginger and aubergine strips to the
pan. Pour over the soy sauce, sherry
and chilli sauce, stir well and cook
for 2 minutes.

Spoon into a warmed serving dish,
sprinkle with chillies and serve
immediately.
Serves 4 to 6

Braised Bamboo Shoots

6 Chinese dried
    mushrooms*
2 tablespoons oil
1 piece root ginger*,
    shredded
2 cloves garlic, sliced
6 spring onions,
    sliced
2 green chillies,
    seeded and
    chopped
1 x 500 g (1 lb) can
    bamboo shoots*,
    drained and sliced
2 tablespoons light
    soy sauce*
2 tablespoons dry
    sherry
125 g (4 oz) cooked
    lean ham, shredded

Soak the mushrooms in warm water
for 15 minutes. Squeeze dry, discard
the hard stalks and slice the
mushroom caps.

Heat the oil in a wok or deep
frying pan, add the ginger, garlic,
spring onions and chillies and stir-fry
for 1 minute. Stir in the remaining
ingredients, mixing well, and cook
for 3 minutes.

Pile into a warmed serving dish
and serve immediately.
Serves 4 to 6

DESSERTS

Deep-Fried Sweet Potato Balls

500 g (1 lb) sweet
  potatoes
125 g (4 oz) rice
  flour
50 g (2 oz) soft
  brown sugar
125 g (4 oz)
  crystallized fruit,
  chopped
50 g (2 oz) sesame
  seeds*, lightly
  toasted
oil for deep-frying

Cook the potatoes in boiling water for 20 minutes until tender; drain and remove the peel. Mash the flesh and gradually beat in the flour and sugar. Stir in the crystallized fruit.

With dampened hands, roll the mixture into walnut-sized balls, then coat with sesame seeds.

Heat the oil in a wok or deep-fryer and deep-fry the potato balls for 5 to 7 minutes, until golden brown. Drain on kitchen paper. Serve hot.

Serves 4 to 6

Walnut Sweet

125 g (4 oz) shelled
  walnuts
3 tablespoons oil
75 g (3 oz) dates,
  stoned
900 ml (1 ½ pints)
  water
150 g (5 oz) sugar
40 g (1 ½ oz)
  ground rice,
  blended with 3
  tablespoons milk
apple flower* to
  decorate

Soak the walnuts in boiling water for 10 minutes, drain and remove the skins; dry on kitchen paper.

Heat the oil in a wok or deep frying pan, add the walnuts and fry quickly until lightly browned (take care not to burn them). Drain on kitchen paper.

Grind the nuts and dates in a blender or fine mincer. Bring the water to the boil and stir in the nut mixture, sugar and blended rice. Bring back to the boil, stirring, and cook for 2 minutes until thickened.

Spoon into a warmed serving dish, decorate with an apple flower and serve hot.

Serves 4 to 6

Caramel Apples

2 egg whites
6 tablespoons
   self-raising flour
4 large dessert
   apples, peeled,
   cored, and each cut
   into 8 pieces
plain flour for
   coating
oil for deep-frying
CARAMEL COATING:
175 g (6 oz) sugar
3 tablespoons water
25 g (1 oz) unsalted
   butter
1-2 tablespoons
   sesame seeds*,
   lightly toasted

Lightly beat the egg whites, then beat in the flour to form a smooth batter. Sprinkle a little plain flour over the apple slices, then coat with batter.

Heat the oil in a wok or deep-fryer and deep-fry the apples for about 5 to 7 minutes, until golden brown. Drain on kitchen paper.

To make the caramel coating, put the sugar and water in a heavy pan and stir over gentle heat until dissolved. Add the butter, increase the heat and continue stirring until the sugar has caramelized to a golden colour. Add the sesame seeds and apples and stir quickly until the apples are well coated with caramel.

Dip the apples into cold water to harden the caramel, drain and serve immediately.
Serves 4

Water Chestnut Cake

150 g (5 oz) water
   chestnut flour*,
   sifted
350 ml (12 fl oz)
   water
500 g (1 lb) canned
   water chestnuts*,
   well drained and
   chopped
50 g (2 oz) unsalted
   butter
150 ml (¼ pint)
   milk
250 g (8 oz) caster
   sugar

Put the flour in a bowl and gradually beat in the water to form a smooth batter.

Put the water chestnuts, butter, milk and sugar in a large pan and bring to the boil. Remove from the heat and stir in half the batter. Bring back to the boil, stirring. Remove from the heat and add the remaining batter. Return to the boil and cook, stirring, for 30 seconds.

Pour into a lined and greased 18 cm (7 inch) square shallow cake tin and cover with greaseproof paper and foil, securing with string. Steam over high heat for 25 to 30 minutes until firm. Leave to cool in the tin.

Turn out and cut into diamond shapes. Arrange on a serving plate and decorate with strawberry slices.
Serves 4 to 6

Fruit Custard

3 eggs
4 tablespoons caster
   sugar
300 ml (½ pint)
   water
350 g (12 oz)
   pineapple
50 g (2 oz) dates
125 g (3 oz)
   crystallized fruit
25 g (1 oz) dried figs
1 tablespoon arrowroot
   or cornflour

Beat the eggs, 1 tablespoon sugar
and 4 tablespoons of the water
together in a deep ovenproof dish.
Place in a steamer and steam for 7 to
8 minutes until the mixture is set.

Shred the pineappple, dates,
crystallized fruit and figs finely. Mix
all the fruit together and spoon over
the egg custard.

Mix the arrowroot or cornflour
and remaining sugar together, then
gradually blend in the water. Bring
the mixture to the boil, stirring, and
cook for 2 minutes. Spoon over the
fruit and serve hot or cold.
Serves 4

Eight Jewel Rice Pudding

350 g (12 oz) short-
    grain pudding rice
4 tablespoons caster
    sugar
50 g (2 oz) unsalted
    butter
125 g (4 oz) glacé
    cherries
50 g (2 oz)
    crystallized orange
    peel
25 g (1 oz) angelica
25 g (1 oz) walnuts
25 g (1 oz) whole
    blanched almonds
50 g (2 oz) seedless
    raisins
5 tablespoons sweet
    red bean paste*
SUGAR SYRUP:
300 ml (½ pint)
    water
50 g (2 oz) sugar
few drops of almond
    essence

Rinse the rice, drain and put in a pan with enough water to cover. Simmer for 15 minutes; drain. Stir in the sugar and half the butter. Chop the cherries, peel, angelica and nuts.

Use remaining butter to grease a 900 ml (1½ pint) pudding basin, then line with a thin layer of rice. Press a little of each fruit and nut into this in a decorative pattern. Mix remaining rice, fruit and nuts. Spoon alternate layers of this mixture and bean paste into the basin, finishing with the rice mixture. Press down firmly.

Cover basin with greaseproof paper and foil, making a pleat in the centre; secure with string. Steam for 1 to 1¼ hours.

To make the syrup, bring the water and sugar to the boil, stirring. Remove from heat and add the almond essence.

Turn the pudding out onto a warmed serving dish and serve hot, with the sugar syrup.
Serves 6

Almond Fruit Salad

4 dessert apples, cored
4 peaches, skinned
    and stoned
125 g (4 oz)
    strawberries
4 slices pineapple
125 g (4 oz) lychees,
    skinned
ALMOND SYRUP:
2 tablespoons ground
    almonds
450 ml (¾ pint)
    water
1 tablespoon cornflour,
    blended with 2
    tablespoons water
3 tablespoons sugar

First, make the syrup. Put the almonds, water, blended cornflour and sugar in a pan and mix well. Gradually bring to the boil, stirring, then simmer for 10 minutes, stirring constantly. Remove from the heat and leave to cool, stirring occasionally to prevent a skin forming.

Slice the apples, peaches and strawberries; cut the pineapple into cubes. Put all the fruit in a bowl and mix well. Spoon over the almond syrup and chill before serving.
Serves 4 to 6

INDEX

Acknowledgments

Photography by Paul Williams
Food prepared by Caroline Ellwood
Photographic stylist: Penny Markham